**Practical Handbook
No 10**

Recording medieval floor tiles

J Stopford

**1990
Council for British Archaeology**

Published 1990 by the Council for British Archaeology
112 Kennington Rd, London SE11 6RE

Copyright © 1990 J Stopford
and Council for British Archaeology *all rights reserved*

British Library Cataloguing in Publication Data
Stopford, J. (Jennie)
 Recording medieval floor tiles, — (Practical handbooks in archaeology, 0951–6117, no. 10)
 1. Paving tiles. Archaeological investigation
 I. Title II. Council for British Archaeology III. Series 738.6

ISBN 1 872414 03 6

Typeset by TOMES. Leamington Spa.
Print by TOMES. Leamington Spa.

Contents

List of figures..iii

List of plates..iv

Acknowledgements..iv

1 Introduction..1

2 General points on recording..5

3 Recording..12

4 Publication..36

5 References..40

List of figures

Fig 1   Measuring a square tile

Fig 2   Measuring a triangle

Fig 3   Measuring fragments

Fig 4   Template showing vertical and 7° angles for recording the angle of bevel

Fig 5   Plain floor tile recording form

Fig 6   A visual comparison chart for percentage estimations

Fig 7   Section of a tile showing 'pared' lower edges

Fig 8   Section of a tile showing 'rebated' lower surface

Fig 9   Plan and section of a scooped key

Fig 10 Decorated floor tile recording form

Fig 11 Mosaic floor tile recording form

Fig 12 Comparison of drawing techniques

List of plates

Pl 1   Stamped and slipped tile, scored diagonally before firing but unbroken

Pl 2   Stamped and slipped tile split from a scored square

Pl 3   A hand incised tile

Pl 4   Hand incised tiles

Pl 5   Hexagonal tile inlaid with white clay

Pl 6   Two-plane relief decorated tile

Pl 7   Two-plane counter relief tile

Pl 8   Line impressed fragment

Pl 9   Stamped and slipped tile made with a cracked stamp

Pl 10 Tiles decorated with the same design and probably made with the same stamp but belonging to different production groups

Pl 11 Stamped and slipped tile with smeared design

Acknowledgements

I am grateful to the Directors of Bordesley Abbey Excavations, in particular Susan Wright and Grenville Astill, and to Richard Morris of the Council for British Archaeology, for their support in the compilation of this guide. I am also grateful for discussions with Ross Dallas of the English Heritage Photogrammetric Unit, University of York, Caroline Jamfrey of the West Yorkshire Archaeological Service, Ellen Walsh of Bordesley Abbey Excavations and the Academic and Specialist Publications Illustrators of English Heritage, especially Karen Guffogg. Tile design drawings are by Karen Guffogg, all other illustrations are by the author.

1 Introduction

1.1 Introduction

This guide is primarily intended for the non-specialist faced with the problem of sorting, recording and compiling reports on ceramic floor tiles. The material may either be from excavations, *in situ*, or in museum or other collections. The guide should be useful for Finds' Assistants, Unit staff, Project Managers, students or amateurs collating material for their own interest or for the *Census of Medieval Tiles*.

Medieval floor tiles are of great value to the archaeologist and historian. This is partly because they have survived in large numbers from a variety of sites scattered all over Britain and the continent, and also because they carry a great deal of accessible information. Like other ceramics, tile fabrics can be analysed, grouped, and possible clay sources identified. In addition, the wide variety of manufacturing and decorative techniques allow detailed characterisation of their production. The impression of the wooden stamps, which were often used in the manufacture of decorated tiles, can frequently be individually identified. The use of the same stamps suggests close links between tiles at different sites. Where a crack has developed across one of these stamps, the sequence of their manufacture is also apparent. An example of a wooden stamp, used in tile production in the late 17th or 18th century, is published by Eames (1980, I, pl viiib). Another example from Winchester Museum is illustrated in Ponsonby and Ponsonby (1934, 26).

The possibility of such close identification of different groups, and the links between them, should allow new insights into what may have been a fairly typical small medieval industry. Comparison of different groups of tiles shows variation in the structure and organisation of the industry, particularly where kiln sites are also known. Where chronological differentiation is sufficient, it is also possible to see how the industry changed as time passed. And since ceramic floor tiles are most frequently found in large, high status buildings such as royal and monastic sites, they can assist in the interpretation of the roles of patrons and users of such buildings in relation to the local economy, and changes that occurred within it. Relative standards of workmanship, the introduction of new and perhaps personalised motifs, the reuse of old tiles or the imitation of old designs, can all show fluctuations in the ideas, aspirations and fortunes of these communities.

In order to make the most of this potential — to allow the reliable identification and interpretation of spatial and chronological differences — it is necessary to be able to make accurate comparisons between data from different sites and periods. This calls for a standardised methodology in recording. It is the purpose of this handbook to indicate what such a system should involve.

1.2 Devising the recording system

An assessment has been made of those characteristics which are useful in showing differences between groups of tiles (Stopford 1990). This was done by recording every conceivable aspect of a sample of *c* 1000 decorated tiles from the site of Bordesley Abbey, Redditch, Hereford & Worcester. The sample included 166 tiles of 57 different designs found *in situ* on five consecutive floors in the abbey church, dating from the early 13th century through to the dissolution in 1538. It was hoped that comparison of the characteristics of the tiles from different floors would give an indication of which aspects were useful in showing changes in tile production and use, and should therefore be retained in the recording system. Likewise, a comparison of characteristics of tiles which occurred together on a floor was used to suggest which of these were helpful in showing differences in the production of tiles in use at the same time.

The results of these tests, together with later work on tiles of all types in Yorkshire, form the basis of the proposed recording system.

1.3 Grouping tiles

Interpretations of medieval tiles as indicators of the structure and organisation of an industry can only be made by comparing one group of tiles with another. Hence the first aim in recording tiles is to assign them to groups. In order to do this it is important to have a clear idea of what these groups represent.

Tiles should be grouped to distinguish between those made at different times or different ways. The tiles in each group should be thought sufficiently similar to one another for their manufacture to have been subject to the same organisational constraints. For example, tiles within a group should not only have been made by the same person or people, or within the same industry, but also have been manufactured using similar processes. A group of people working together might make significant changes to their methods of manufacture at different times. Tiles which were the products of the various forms of organisation adopted would belong to separate groups, even though the people making them were the same. Groups formed along these lines may be called *production groups*.

Decorated tiles have often been grouped by design, using terms such as '9-tile designs', 'single repeating designs', *etc*. The Bordesley analysis, however, suggests that groups defined by design bear no relation to tiles of different workshops. The Canynges pavement, published in the British Museum catalogue (Eames 1980, I, pl vii) also shows that the centre four tiles of a 12-tile pattern were sometimes used on their own. This method has consequently been discarded. Designs used together to create a 4-, 9-, 12- or 16-tile design are linked by the design number system (see below page 23).

Successful grouping depends upon taking several different characteristics together, rather than concentrating exclusively on one aspect of tiles, such as design. The relevant characteristics will vary from group to group. One of the production groups from Bordesley Abbey, for example, is mainly characterised by design: all the tiles are heraldic. However, there are other heraldic tiles from the site which do not belong to this production group. The two groups can be distinguished by also taking into account their dimensions, the angle of bevel of the tile sides, the standard of their decoration, and the degree of oxidisation of the tile fabric.

Plain, decorated and mosaic groups

These are the conventional broad divisions of different types of floor tiles. Although these divisions are to a large extent quite arbitrary, they are retained here for recording purposes because slightly different recording categories apply to each type.

For the purposes of this recording system, *plain floor tiles* (**PFT**) are square, triangular or (rarely) rectangular, whose upper surface has either been entirely covered with slip and then glazed, or whose upper surface has been glazed without slip. *Decorated floor tiles* (**DFT**) are usually square, triangular or rectangular and have a design on the upper surface. *Mosaic tiles* (**MFT**) are those which make a pattern by virtue of their interlocking shapes. They may or may not have a design on the upper surface. It is important to understand that production groups may cross-cut the divisions imposed by the recording system. Decorated tiles are, for example, usually found together with plain ones; both could therefore belong to the same production group. Plain tiles are often used alongside and as part of the same pavement as elaborate mosaic panels, and it has already been noted that mosaic tiles may also be decorated. When assigning tiles to production groups it is, therefore, important to remember that the plain/mosaic/decorated divisions of the recording system may be quite artificial. Where more than one type of tile is being recorded, use the same fabric code, design number and stamp number series throughout.

Recording individual tiles and groups of tiles

In what circumstances should tiles be recorded individually? Or can they be assigned to groups by eye, and the group recorded as a whole? These are difficult questions. In general it is suggested that tiles should be recorded individually when:

a the tiles are decorated: because it is important to know which tiles were definitely made using the same stamps (see pages 21–2 for a discussion of stamps). This demands an individual record. For the same reason, decorated tiles need to be numbered and stored in sequence, so that they are retrievable
b the recorder lacks experience
c only a comparatively small number of tiles is involved. But, where a sufficient number (see below) of plain or mosaic tiles has been recorded individually to establish the characteristics of a production group, subsequent tiles can be added to that group without individual recording so long as they conform in all respects.

Whichever approach is taken, the policy followed must be clearly stated, and the total numbers of tiles and fragments should be listed for each group.

1.4 Sample size

The validity of statements and interpretations based upon production groups will depend not only on a rigorous methodology, but also upon having a reasonably large sample of tiles. In practice, however, the definition of what constitutes an 'adequate sample' will vary according to the sizes of assemblages recovered, and also the time and resources available to process them. The chief need is always to publish the size of the sample, and to state how the recording was done. Results can then be evaluated accordingly.

1.5 Using computers

The use of computers in recording tiles will depend on the quantity of material involved, the resources available, and the preference of the recorder. There is no point in discussing computerisation in detail as this will vary with circumstance and according to the type of software being used. However, the recording forms and methods set out below are suitable both for use by hand, or adaptation to a database management package. The recording system has been used successfully with both *Dbase* and *Oracle*.

The only computer term which is used here is the word *variable*. A variable is a category of recordable information: for example, the provenance of a tile, the depth of the tile, or the colour of the glaze.

1.6 How the rest of the handbook works

The next section provides background information on how to record different types of variables. This is intended to provide basic information relevant to recording all types of tiles in a manner which is not only accurate and consistent, but also quick. It is, of course, impossible for any recording scheme to cover every eventuality; nevertheless, it is hoped that the rationale behind the system will enable individual recorders to solve problems or deal with omissions as they arise.

Section 3 sets out sample recording forms for plain, decorated, and mosaic tiles, with instructions for filling in data for each category. Section 4 provides guidelines for publishing results of tile recording and drawing tile designs.

2 General Points on Recording

2.1 Descriptive variables

The categories considered here are descriptions of glazes, fabrics, shape, surface treatments, faults in manufacture, keys, and decorative techniques.

The main difficulty with descriptive variables is the problem of standardisation. This applies particularly to the description of different decorative techniques. Many of the explanations for different decorative characteristics are still conjectural, and it is the *characteristics*, rather than the assumed explanations, which must be recorded. So when the recorder encounters descriptive variables which are not listed in the recording section, it is important that as far as possible the terms be defined using drawings and quantification.

With this said, it is a mistake to spend too much time agonizing over how to describe very *unusual characteristics*. The point of standardising the recording of large numbers of artefacts is to allow their similarities and differences to be more easily recognised. An unusual aspect of a group of tiles, such as a hand incised decorative technique (discussed on page 21), will be immediately distinguishable. Most of the time it will be enough to know that all the tiles are hand incised. If there are clear differences in the exact incision technique used on one tile and another, the number of tiles involved will usually be small enough to sort out later.

A further risk is the danger of making *unwarranted assumptions*. It cannot be assumed that tiles which share the same designs will be similar in any other respect. There is, for example, an inlaid and relief decorated version of a single design from Bordesley Abbey (for definitions of these terms see pages 19–20). The relief version of this has been published as a square tile in the Bordesley Abbey II report (Hirst, Walsh & Wright 1983, 155, A3), while the inlaid version published in the British Museum catalogue is rectangular (Eames 1980, II, design 1290). In fact there is only a single fragment of the relief version, which has just been assumed to be square (S Wright pers comm).

Recording fabrics by eye

Peacock (1977, 21–33) provides the standard guide to describing fabrics. However, this is the most difficult of the descriptive variables to record quickly and consistently. It should be noted that a recent comparison of visual fabric recording and scientific fabric analysis suggests that, where there are no very distinctive inclusions, visually recorded fabrics may only show archaeologically useful distinctions at the broadest possible level (Stopford 1990). This has consequences for the possibilities of interpreting these data, and suggests that a great deal of time should not be spent on this category. If there is a very clear difference between fabric types this will quickly become apparent. If not, it is unlikely that visually recorded distinctions will be very useful.

In summary, the important needs in recording descriptive variables are to:
a quantify descriptions where possible
b record characteristics as they appear on the tile rather than according to their assumed causes
c be explicit about uncertain cases
d be consistent

The importance of (c) is stressed: if the recorder does not know the answer to a question (s)he should enter '***Don't Know***'. Where the answer to a question is ambiguous, record both possibilities with an oblique sign (/) between them. Where two or more answers to a question are true, record them all with a 'plus' sign (+) in between.

2.2 Quantative variables

Categories involved here are tile dimensions, angle of bevel, and nail holes. All actual measurements are made in millimetres (mm).

Recording tile dimensions is simple to do but difficult to explain. The main points to remember are these:
a all measurements must be repeatable; exactly the same thing must be measured each time, so that measurements are comparable
b there must be a clear idea of what exactly is being measured; measurements should only be taken where there are easily definable points

The consequence of these points is that only 'complete' measurements are recorded. What, in the case of tiles of various shapes and fragments of various sizes, constitutes 'complete' measurements, is discussed below.

Depth

Depth is recorded for all fragments/tiles regardless of shape, unless they have spalled (*ie*, fractured on the horizontal plane) and the depth is therefore incomplete.

Squares and rectangles

The complete surface measurements taken on a square or rectangular tile are shown in Figure 1. Note that measurements are taken across the body of the tile rather than along the edges, because the corners of tiles are often chipped.

Triangles

Most triangular tiles are made from scored and split squares (see Pls 1 and 2). It is therefore important to measure the same dimensions on the triangles as on the squares. This means measuring along the tile sides, as shown in Figure 2. It should be noted, however, that the dimensions of triangles will often be slightly smaller than the square tiles of the groups to which they belong, because of chipped corners. There seems no solution to this, except to bear it in mind when grouping tiles.

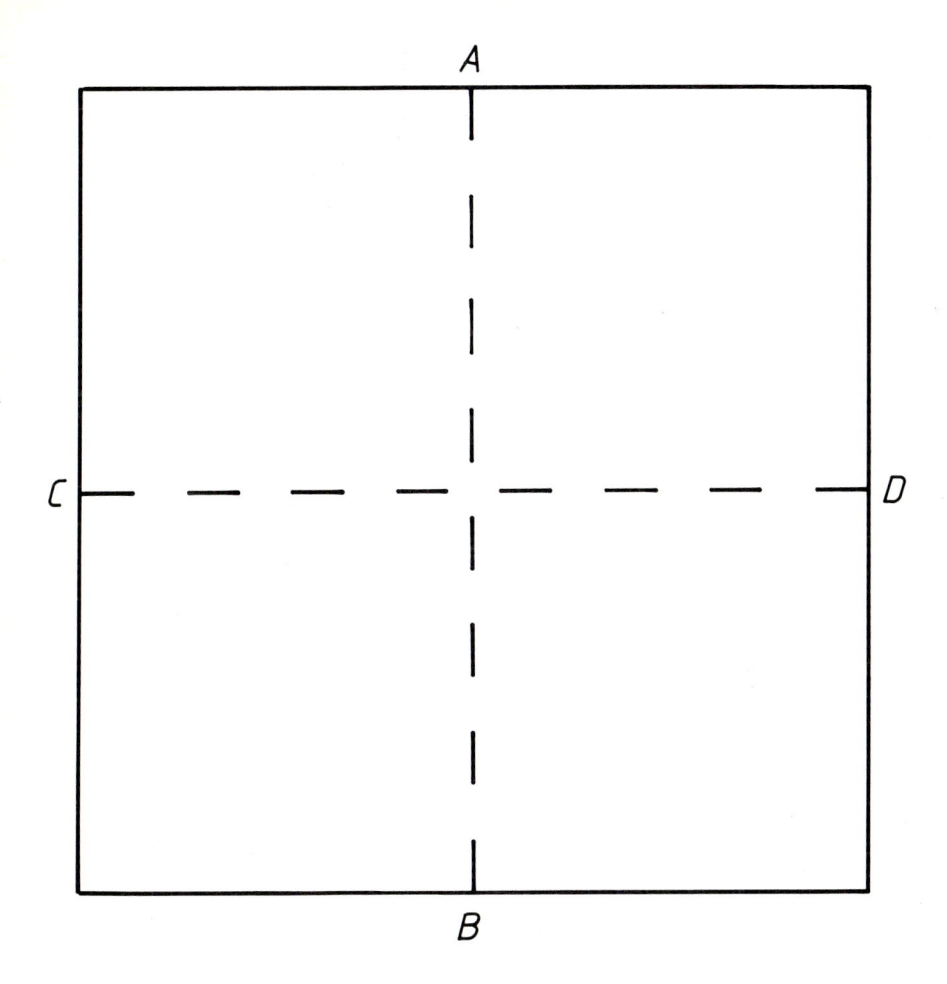

Fig 1 Measuring a square tile: the two complete dimensions are AB and CD

Whenever the dimension being measured is variable, for example the depth of the tile is uneven, take an average point.

Mosaic shapes

Unlike the tiles so far discussed, mosaic shapes do not have easily definable points for taking measurements. The coded templates in the British Museum catalogue (Eames 1980, II, S1-S328) are therefore used instead. See page 29 for details.

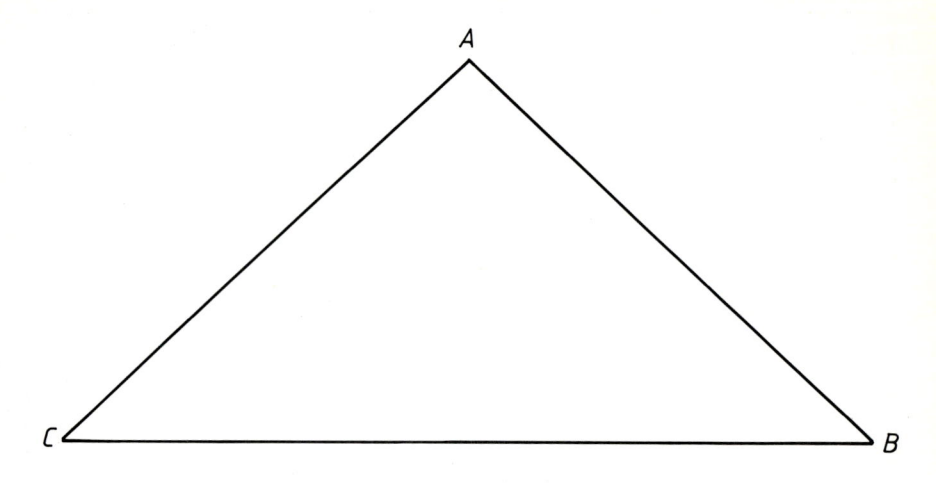

Fig 2 *Measuring a triangle: the two complete dimensions are AB and AC*

Fragments

Fragments are here defined as pieces of tile whose only complete dimension is depth. Tiles with one other complete dimension (*eg*, either the length or breadth of a square tile) are not, therefore, classed as fragments. Among mosaic tiles, whose dimensions are measured using templates, any tile which does not form a complete 'shape' (see above) is classed as a fragment.

Since fragments have no repeatable upper surface measurements, only their depth is recorded by direct measurement. However, some record is also needed of their approximate size, and a coded template is used (Fig 3, template in back pocket). This is a 'not more than' measure of the surface area of the fragment. Where the fragment is irregularly shaped, estimate the relevant code.

Other quantative variables

Angle of bevel

The angle of bevel can vary on all four sides of a single square tile. However, some groups of tiles do have consistently vertical, or consistently steeply bevelled sides. The angle of bevel is therefore only recorded as either vertical, slightly bevelled (*ie*, less than 7°), or steeply bevelled (*ie*, more than 7°). Figure 4 shows a 7° angle and tiles can be measured against this. With practice this category can be recorded by eye (template based on Fig 7 in back pocket).

Nail holes

These are small holes found in the upper surface of some tiles (see Pl 3). They are thought to have been made from the points of nails, hammered through a wooden template or stamp, in order to hold the clay firmly during manufacture.

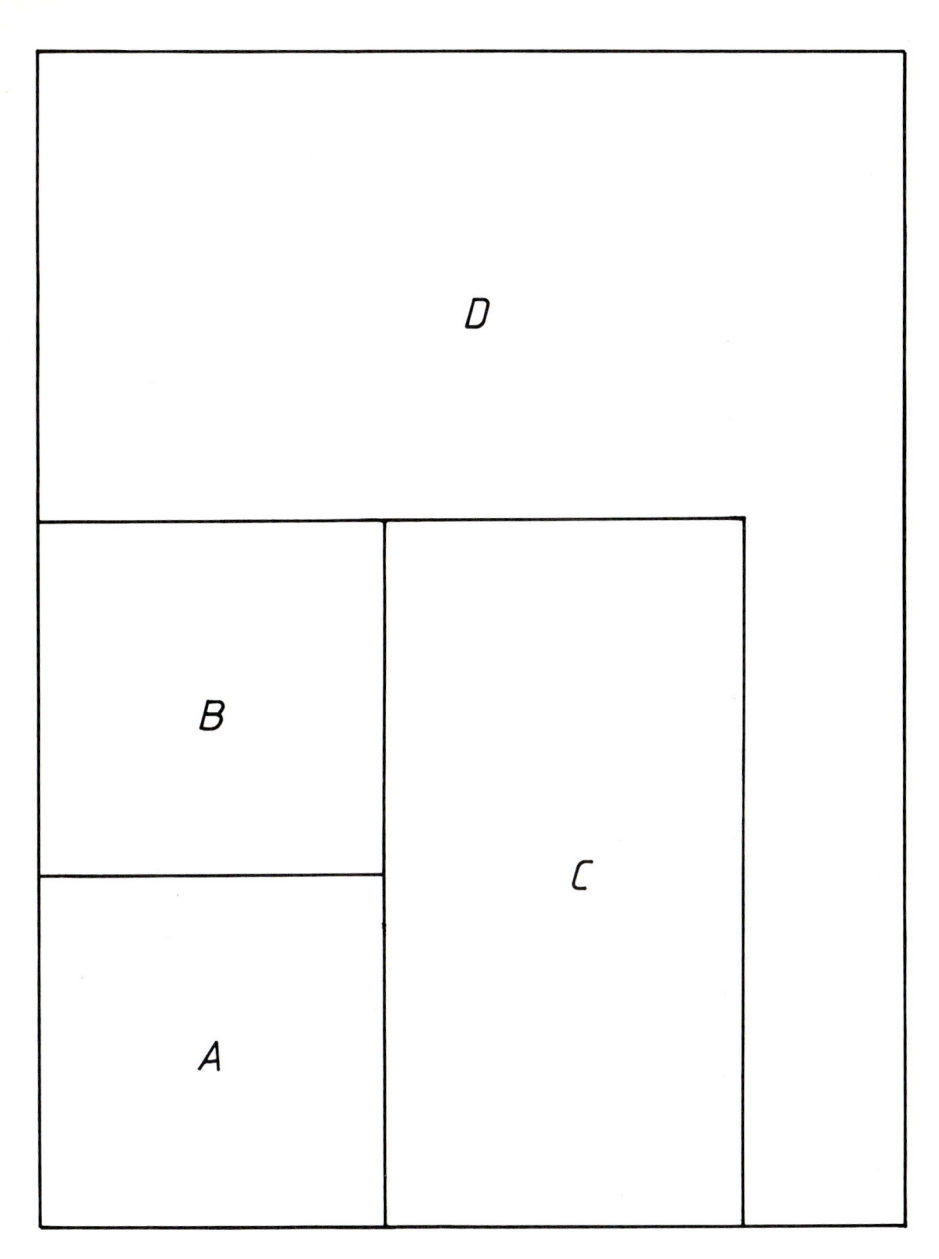

Fig 3 Measuring fragments: use the appropriate code to indicate a 'not more than' measure of the surface area of a fragment (a full size template is in back pocket)

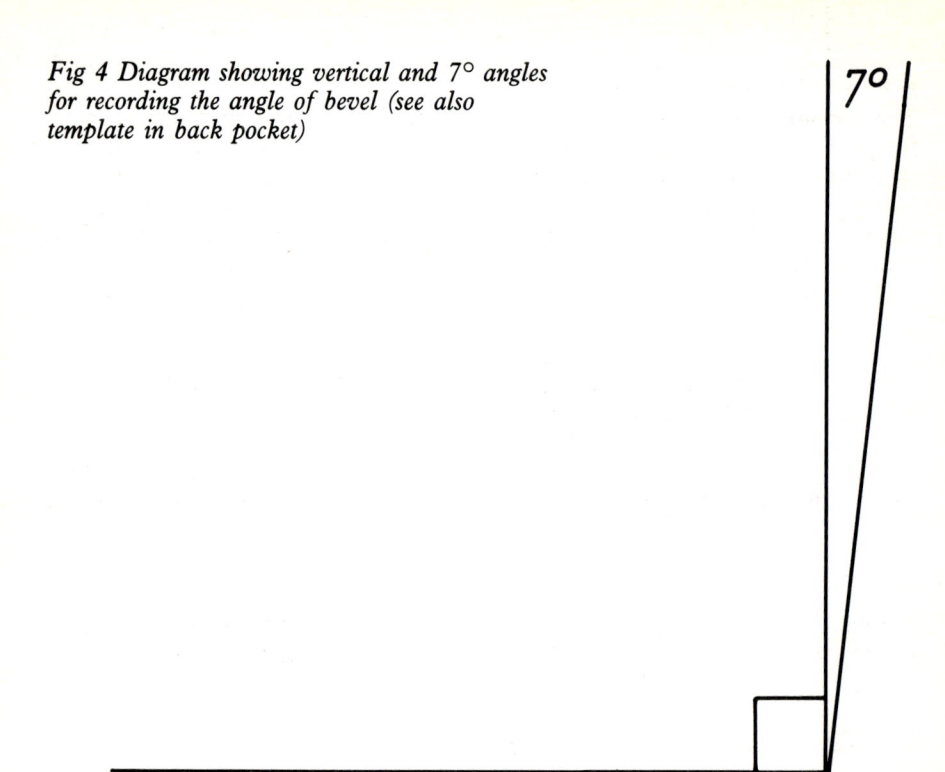

Fig 4 Diagram showing vertical and 7° angles for recording the angle of bevel (see also template in back pocket)

Nail holes are not always easy to recognise; they can be confused with voids in the tile fabric. However, they often have slip and/or glaze in them, as they were made before the slip and glaze were applied to the tile. They are more common on plain than decorated tiles, and have been found in various configurations: for example, in all four corners of tiles, in diagonal corners only, and in the centre. Record the number and arrangement of nail holes on a tile or fragment, and the distance between the nail holes and the corners of the tile. Since the corners of tiles are often chipped, and since the distance of nail holes from tile corners can vary on one tile, there is no point trying to be over precise. The range of the greatest and smallest distance is all that need be recorded, and all measurements may be rounded to the nearest 5mm.

Among mosaic tiles 'corners' are not easily defined. The distance measured is from the nail holes to the nearest unbroken tile edge.

The important rules when quantifying variables are to:
a use actual measurements only where these are repeatable
b record complete measurements only
c do not waste time where precision is unattainable
d use ranges where necessary
e use templates where possible
f do not use the < and > signs — they are often confused

2.3 Qualitative variables

The categories concerned here are assessments of wear and fragment size. Fragment size has been discussed above. Wear is recorded by grading from 1 to 4, where 1 applies to the least worn tiles, and 4 to the most. The tiles used in the plates have been graded for wear by way of examples, and guidelines for recording wear are given in the relevant sections of the recording forms. The value of recording these characteristics is as a check on the validity of the other variables. It is easy to forget the limitations of the data once the actual tiles are no longer in view. If, for example, nail holes are recorded on only some of the tiles in what otherwise looks like a production group, this might be explained if the tiles without nail holes are also those with wear grades of 4. Likewise, where decorated tiles at two different sites are recorded as made using the same stamps, but one of these is recorded as fragment size A, the value of this information is put into perspective. However, the most common mistake is to assume that very worn tiles were never decorated. Tiles with wear grade 4 recorded as plain floor tiles may once have been decorated.

2.4 Tiles *in situ*

Where tiles have been reset, or are still *in situ*, many variables cannot be recorded. Record whatever is possible, plus the arrangement of the tiles in relation to each other.

2.5 Tiles from excavations

Where tiles from stratified excavations are being recorded, some additional variables may be useful. Lower surface measurements may be needed for matching loose tiles with tile impressions in a stratified floor. The presence of more than one type of mortar on tile bases can also be useful as a possible indication that a tile, or group of tiles, has been reused.

3 Recording

The recording of plain, decorated and mosaic tiles is set out separately in the following sections. Each section is organised in a similar way. Any points particular to the type of tile being recorded are discussed at the beginning of the section. Then each category on the form is listed, with an expansion of the question being asked, a cross reference to the general points in Section 2 above, and instructions on how to fill it in.

Although there is considerable overlap between the three recording forms, they are set out separately to avoid confusion, and for speedy use. Each form is organised in the same way, dealing first with general aspects and dimensions, then with all aspects of the upper surface, then the sides, then the base of the tile — so that each tile only has to be turned round and over once. Abbreviations, for quick recording, are given as bold capitals (*eg*, **TRI**angle). Stick to these as far as possible. Make a note in the back of the book of any additional recording abbreviations you use. A4 size templates of the recording forms (Figs 5, 10 and 11) are included in the pocket inside the back cover, from which they may be removed and copied as required.

The next section deals with recording plain tiles. Turn to page 18 to record decorated tiles. Turn to page 28 to record mosaic tiles.

3.1 Plain floor tiles

Notes on using the recording form for plain tiles (Fig 5)
1 *Site*: The site where the tiles were found.
2 *Provenance now*: Where the tiles are now stored. If they are *in situ*, give their whereabouts in the building: *eg*, **S**outh Transept. Keep a record of any abbreviations used.
3 *Number of tiles* described by this record. See notes on page 3 on recording tiles individually or not. Where the record is of an individual tile, put **1**. Where the record is for a group of tiles put the number of whole tiles and the number of fragments.
4 *Group Number:* The production group number. See notes on pages 2–3 on assigning tiles to production groups. Leave blank if a group number has not yet been allocated. Record: **Production Group 1, PG2, PG3**.
5 *Context/Phasing*: Record any contextual information here. If the tile was found *in situ*, record as **IS**.

Shape and size (see general points on pages 6–8).
6 *Shape*: What shape was/is the complete tile? Record: **SQ**uare, **TRI**angle, **REC**tangle, **D**on't **K**now. Put **D**on't **K**now if there is not enough of the tile present to be certain of the shape — for example that it is definitely a square and not a rectangle.

1. SITE _____   2. PROVENANCE NOW _____
3. NUMBER OF TILES _____   4. GROUP NUMBER _____
5. CONTEXT/PHASING _____

Shape and Size

6. SHAPE _____   7. DEPTH _____   8. FRAG _____
9. USLONG _____   10. USSHORT _____   11. USONE _____

Upper Surface

12. SLIP _____   13. GLAZE _____
14. SCORED _____   15. SPLIT _____
16. NAIL HOLES _____   17. DISTANCE _____
18. DAMAGE _____   19. WEAR _____

Sides and Core

20. ANGLE OF BEVEL _____   21. FABRIC CODE _____
22. FIRING _____

Lower Surface

22. SANDY _____   23. KEYS _____

Comments: _____
_____

Fig 5 Plain floor tile recording form (see also template in back pocket)

7   *Depth*: Record the depth of the tile in mm. Depth can be recorded for all except spalled fragments. Where the depth of the tile is uneven, choose an average point.
8   *Fragment Code*: Tiles with depth as their only complete measurement are given a fragment code. This is a 'not more than' measure of the surface area of the fragment. Codes for different sized fragments are given in Figure 3. Where the fragment is irregularly shaped, estimate the relevant code. Record: **A, B, C,** *etc.*
9   *Upper Surface Long*: Give the longer complete upper surface measurement, if there is one, in mm.
10 *Upper Surface Short*: Give the shorter complete upper surface measurement, if there is one, in mm.
11 *Upper Surface One*: Where there is only one complete measurement, put it here.

Upper surface
12 *Slip*: Slip is defined here as a layer of white clay on the upper surface of the tile. Record: **Y**es + depth of slip in mm, **N**o, **D**on't **K**now. Put **D**on't **K**now if the tile is worn down to the quarry (*ie*, there is no slip or glaze left).
13 *Glaze*: What colour has the glaze on the upper surface of the tile fired to? Record: **BL**ack, **BR**own, **C**ream, **G**reen **D**ark, **G**reen **L**ight, **OL**ive, **OR**ange, **P**urple brown, **Y**ellow, **D**on't **K**now.
    These abbreviations follow Eames' catalogue of tiles in the British Museum (1980, I, 286). Be wary of using **C**ream; check that the slip does not just look cream because the glaze has worn off. Put **D**on't **K**now if the tile is too worn to tell the colour of the glaze. If the tile is streaked or spotted so that more than one colour is present, put both: *eg*, **Y+BR** or **Y+GL**, *etc.*
14 *Scored*: Has the upper surface of the tile been cut part way through the depth of the tile? See Plate 1. Record: **Y**es, **N**o, **D**on't **K**now.
15 *Split*: Have one or more sides of the tile been scored and broken to make a triangle or small square or small rectangle? See Plate 2. Record: **Y**es, **N**o, **D**on't **K**now.
16 *Nail holes*: Are there any nail holes in the corners or centre of the tile? See the general points on pages 8 – 10 and Plate 3 for information on how to record and recognise nail holes. Record the number of holes, whether they are in adjacent or diagonal corners, and/or the centre of the tile. For example: **1COR**ner, **2ADJ**acent, **2DIA**gonal, **3ADJ**acent + **1CEN**tre, **N**o, **D**on't **K**now. Only record the number of nail holes you can actually see on each tile or fragment. Put **D**on't **K**now if it is not clear.
17 *Distance*: Where there are nail holes in the corner(s) of the tile, give the range of the distance from the corners to the nail holes. See the general points on page 10 for how to record this. Recording examples:
        5 *ie*, the hole/s is/are up to 5mm from the corner
        5 – 10 *ie*, the holes are between 5 and 10mm from the corner
        10 – 25 *ie*, the holes are between 10 and 25mm from the corner

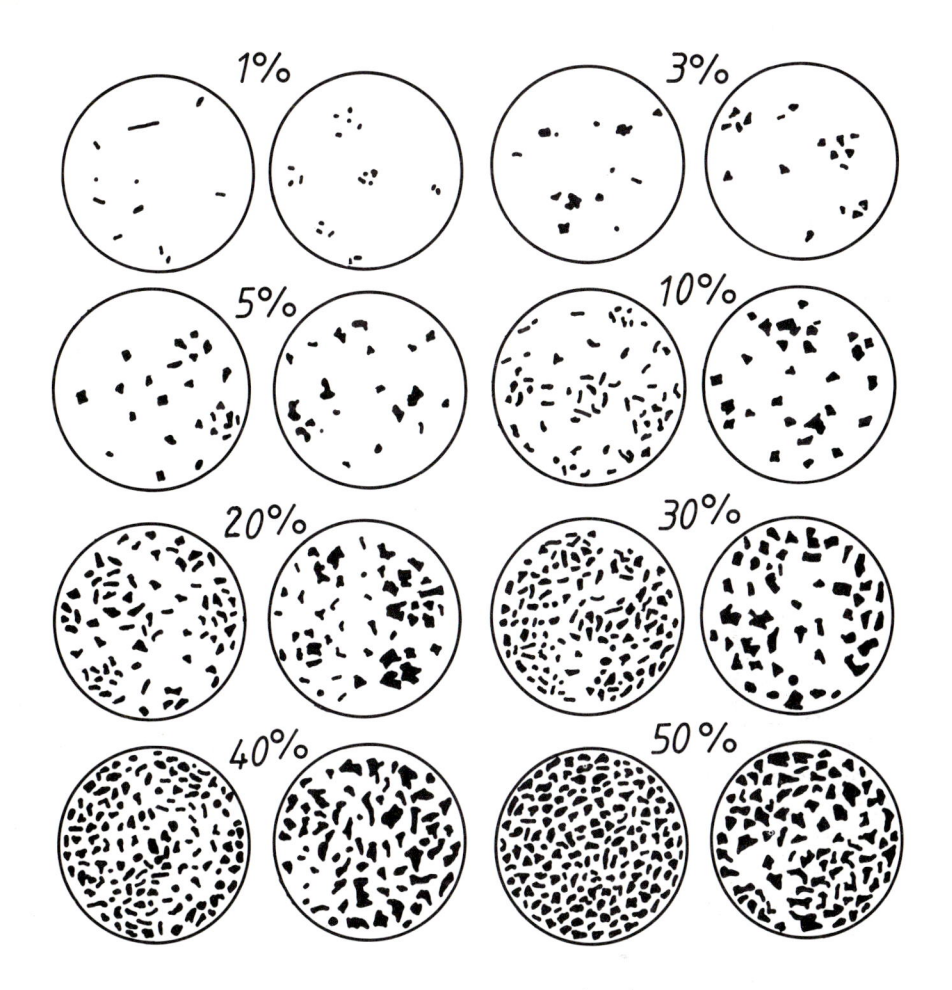

Fig 6 A visual comparison chart for percentage estimations

18 *Damage*: Was the tile damaged in any particular way during its production? Bear the general points on recording descriptive variables in mind (see pages 5–6) when filling in this category; consistency is particularly important. Also see Plate 11. The following are some possible 'damage' categories and abbreviations:

> **UNEVEN** — the upper surface of the quarry is uneven
> **SMEAR**ed — the slip does not cover the whole upper surface
> **BLOT**chy — the glaze has left black spots on the upper surface
> **SAND**y — sand on the upper surface before firing
> **PACK**ing lines — cracks in the fabric which show right through

to the lower surface, suggesting that several lumps of clay have been pressed together
WARPed — the tile is warped
WASTER — the tile is so badly damaged it could not possibly have been used in a floor. Be careful about using this — very poor tiles are known to have been used. The presence of any mortar or wear marks suggesting use should be looked for
None
Don't **K**now

19 Wear: Grade the degree of wear on the tile. Use the following as approximate guidelines to grade wear from 1 to 4, and see the Plates for examples:

- *1* All the slip and more than 75% of the glaze is present on the tile or fragment.
- *2* More than 50% of the glaze and 75% of the slip is present.
- *3* Less than 25% of the glaze, but more than 50% of the slip is present.
- *4* Less than 25% of the slip and no glaze is present.

Sides and Core

20 Angle of bevel: Are the sides of the tile vertical, sloped at less than 7°, or more than 7°? See page 8 for general points. Use Figure 4 (*back pocket*) as a template to check if the angle is more or less than 7°. Record: **VE**rtical, **SL**ightly bevelled (*ie*, less than 7°), **ST**eeply bevelled (*ie*, more than 7°).

21 Fabric code: See notes on page 5. Fabric can only be recorded from tile fragments with a clean, broken edge. Each fabric type should be described as set out below. The allotted fabric code is then used in the recording form. Delete or fill in as applicable:

Fabric Code_____

Texture: LAMINATED/WELL MIXED   Fracture: SMOOTH/JAGGED

Hardness: HARD/AVERAGE/SOFT

Inclusions: **QUARTZ**   SIZE: _____   FREQ: _____

Other: _____ SIZE: _____   FREQ: _____

Other: _____ SIZE: _____   FREQ: _____

Comment: _____

Fabric is *soft* if it can be scratched with a fingernail, *average* if it can be scratched by metal, *hard* if it cannot be scratched by metal. Use the abbreviation **LT** for Less Than, and **MT** for More Than; the symbols < and > are too often confused. Use Figure 6 to estimate frequency and record the relevant percentages. Record inclusion size as a range, in mm. For example: **1-2mm, 1-10mm, Less Than 1mm**, *etc*.

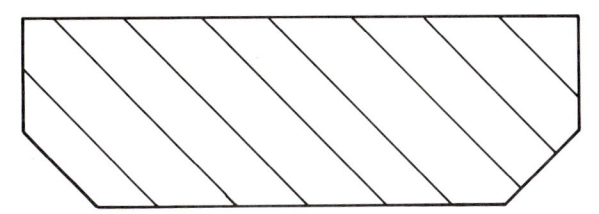

Fig 7 Section of a tile showing 'pared' lower edges

22 **Firing**: Tiles fired in the presence of oxygen are said to be 'oxidised', and their fabric is pink or red. Tiles fired in an atmosphere where oxygen is excluded are said to be 'reduced', and their fabric is grey or black. Many tiles are partly oxidised and partly reduced. Be careful about only recording what you actually know about each tile or fragment. Record:

    OXidised — fabric is red or pink at surfaces and core
    REDuced — fabric is grey or black at surfaces and core
    CORE REDuced — surfaces are oxidised but the core is reduced
    OXidised **SURFaceS** — all surfaces oxidised, core unknown
    Upper Surface **PATCHY** — the upper surface is partly reduced, the rest of the tile sides are oxidised
    Upper Surface **RED**uced — lower surface and sides oxidised, but upper surface reduced
    Don't **K**now

Lower Surface

23 **Sandy**: Has the tile got sand on its base? Record: **Y**es, **N**o, **D**on't **K**now.

24 **Keys**: Have any keys been cut into the lower surface of the tile?
Any part of the lower surface that has been cut away is recorded here. A variety of keys are illustrated by Ponsonby and Ponsonby (1934, 33). The abbreviations used by Eames (1980, I, 286) in the catalogue of tiles in the British Museum are followed here, with one alteration. 'Bevel' is replaced by 'pared' in order to avoid confusion with the bevelled sides in category 24. **Pared** means that the edges of the base of the tile have been cut away as shown in Figure 7, and the number present means the number of edges which are pared in this way. **Rebate** is a piece of clay cut out along one of the base edges (see Fig 8). These are usually restricted to rectangular tiles

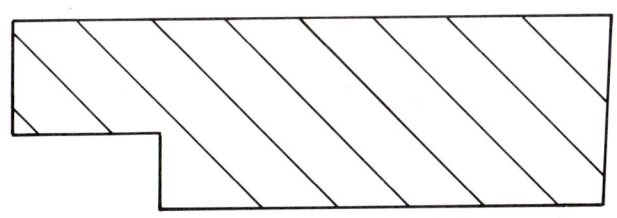

Fig 8 Section of a tile showing 'rebated' lower surface

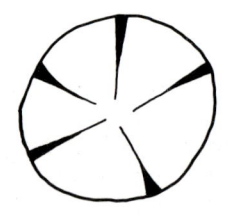

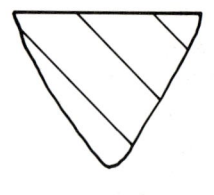

Fig 9 Plan and section of a scooped key

thought to be made for use as step risers. Record as follows and draw a rough sketch of one of the keys in plan and section as, for example, shown in Figure 9.

SCooped + number present
STabbed **R**ound + number present
STabbed **S**quare + number present
PARED + number present
X — a cross is cut in the base of the tile
REBATE
None
Don't **K**now

3.2 Decorated floor tiles

Decorative techniques

A nomenclature has been provided by Eames (1980, I, 17-71) and has been amended and summarized by Norton (1984) in a glossary to the *Tile Census Guidelines*. But problems remain. The distinction between some techniques is unclear, some of the terms are confusing, and the level of detail required in recording has not been discussed.

An attempt has been made here to simplify recording and increase accuracy. The major techniques are described in detail below and illustrated with photographs (see all the Plates). The emphasis is on showing the distinction between one technique and another, and showing how to record them accurately. The unusual techniques are also described, but with some modifications. Where no clear distinction can be drawn between two unusual techniques, or where two techniques are often used together on a tile, they are recorded using a single term. The general notes on recording unusual characteristics, on page 5, are particularly relevant here. Other general points on recording descriptive variables on pages 5–6 are also relevant.

The main decorative techniques

a) Slip decoration and inlaying

By far the most common method of decorating tiles was to use a wooden stamp to impress an imprint of the design onto a part dried quarry. The resulting cavity was then either filled with carefully prepared plastic white clay (inlayed), or the surface of the tile was coated in slip (white clay suspended in liquid) and the slip scraped off the areas not depressed by the stamp (stamped and slipped). The tiles were then glazed and fired.

The distinction between these two techniques has often been confused. Generally tiles with a thin coating of white clay are stamped and slip decorated, while tiles with a thick layer of white clay are inlaid. However, the depth of white clay can vary anywhere between a skin thickness and 5mm, and the borderline between the two techniques is unclear. To avoid this uncertainty, and because depth of white clay can be a good indicator of different workshops, the depth of the white clay should be recorded whenever possible, for both stamped and slipped and inlaid tiles (Pl 10). Record as follows:

Stamped & Slipped + depth of slip in mm.
Inlaid + depth of inlay in mm.
Where it is unclear which of the two techniques has been used, record:
SS/I + depth of white clay in mm.
Where it is clear that a liquid slip has been used in the tile's decoration, but it is not clear whether the quarry was stamped, or whether one of the unusual slip decoration techniques (pages 20–1) are applicable, record:
Slip Decorated + depth of slip in mm.

b) Relief and counter relief

Relief decorated tiles have a raised design on their upper surface. On *counter relief* tiles the design is impressed into the quarry, and the background is raised. Counter relief tiles can, therefore, be just like inlaid tiles but without the inlay. Relief and counter relief tiles can either be slipped and glazed all over the upper surface, or just glazed.

There is a further distinction between *two-plane* and *modelled* relief and counter relief tiles. On two-plane tiles the raised parts have vertical sides, while on modelled tiles the relief decoration is curved. See Plates 6 and 7. Record as:

2 PLANE Relief
MODELled Relief
2 PLANE Counter Relief
MODELled Counter Relief

In practice, most problems arise in distinguishing between relief and counter relief, particularly where two-plane tiles are concerned, because it depends on identifying which plane forms the 'design'. Doubtful cases should be recorded as such; *ie*, **R/CR**. If you do not know whether the tile is two-plane or modelled, just record as **Relief** or **Counter Relief**.

c) Line impressed
These are similar to counter relief tiles in that the design is impressed into the tile quarry, which is then either slipped and glazed, or just glazed, and fired. However on *line impressed* tiles the motif is entirely linear, either giving the effect of an outline, usually of a simple motif, such as a rosette or *fleur-de-lis*, or forming an intricate crisscross design (see Pl 8). This technique is sometimes made using small stamps, and found on mosaic tiles (see section on small stamps on page 29). Record as:

Line IMPressed + depth of impression in mm.

There may be occasions where it is difficult to distinguish between line impressed and counter-relief techniques. As usual, where unsure, put both possibilities; *eg*, **L IMP/CR**.

Unusual techniques
d) Stamp over slip/slip over impression
A distinction has been made between two different methods of stamp and slip decoration (Drury 1979, 9–11). These are known as 'slip-over-impression', which is the slip decoration technique described in (a) above, and 'stamp-over-slip' where Drury suggests the upper surface of the tile was covered in slip before stamping. Drury argues that the different methods can be distinguished by the slip. This is thought to lap up the edges of the stamped impression where the slip was applied after the quarry was stamped, but break at the base of the impression, where the tile was stamped after the slip was applied. In practice, however, the slip-over-impression technique seems to be far more widespread. Record slip-over-impression tiles as stamped and slipped (**SS**), as described in (a) above, unless it is clear that the stamp-over-slip method was used. In that case, record: **S OVER S** + depth of slip in mm.

e) Reverse slip/inlay
The slip and inlay described in all sections above have been made from a white or china clay, and this was used to contrast against a red clay quarry. In rare cases these colours are reversed, with the body fabric either made of, or covered with, a layer of white or pale pink clay, which is subsequently inlaid in red (see Knight & Keen 1977, 65–75 for further details). These are recorded in the same way as the usual slip and inlaid tiles, but are termed 'reverse' slip or 'reverse' inlay. For example:

REVERSE SS + depth of slip in mm.
REVERSE Inlay + depth in mm.

f) Slip Painted
These are slip decorated tiles which were not stamped. The slip forming the design was applied directly onto the upper surface of the tile, sometimes using a brush or squeezed through a nozzle, and sometimes using a stencil. Since all these methods are extremely unusual, there is no need to try to distinguish between

them in the initial stages of recording. In all cases the design will be the highest part of the tile, proud of the upper surface of the quarry. Record as **Slip Painted**.

g) Hand Incised
This term is used here to include all cases where the decoration has involved cutting into, or scraping away at, the upper surface of the tile, by hand. In the past there have been efforts to differentiate between hand incision, combing, and a technique called sgraffiato. In practice the distinctions are unclear, and the techniques are often used in combination on the same tile (see Pls 3 and 4). They are all unusual. Where a particular method of hand incision is used, this can be described in detail later as a group characteristic, with the aid of drawings. Hand incised tiles can be slipped and glazed, with the incision or scraping cutting through the slip to the body fabric, or they can just be glazed. Record hand incised tiles as **Hand INCised**.

Stamps and designs

The main advantage of decorated tiles as archaeological tools is that the great majority are produced using wooden stamps (as described on page 19 above). The same stamp would have been used to produce many tiles, and the distribution of these tiles therefore provides a key to interpreting the structure and organisation of different tile industries. For this reason the accurate identification of tiles made using the same stamps is of the greatest importance. Unfortunately, this is the aspect of tile recording that has led to the greatest confusion in the past because of a failure to distinguish between stamps and design. In particular, the failure to explain whether a comparison is being made between tiles made from the same stamp, or tiles merely of the same design, has caused many problems in tile studies.

The design is the pattern on the upper surface of a tile. A stamp is used to impress this design onto the tile. Several stamps might be made of one design. Because they are cut out of a wooden block, it is likely that they will be slightly different to one another, even when they are good copies of the same design. Identifying tiles made from the same stamp means identifying these slight variations, and a method for doing this is described below.

This section should be read in conjunction with the guide to allocating new design numbers and to drawing designs for publication (pages 36 – 7) so that the different techniques involved are clear.

Identifying tiles made from the same stamps
The use of the same stamp can be identified most easily where a crack has developed across the stamp. This leaves a raised line of clay across the otherwise impressed parts of the tile (see Pl 9). A cracked stamp can sometimes be followed through a number of different stages, which convincingly establishes the relative chronology of the tiles it was used to make.

However, stamps can quite often be identified even where there is no crack — by comparing tracings of stamp impressions on different tiles. This is quite different from drawing designs. Identifying stamps requires a very accurate tracing of those parts of the impression where the edges of the stamp can be clearly seen. This means that the slip, which often does not exactly follow the stamp impression, is ignored, and only the ridges or ledges left by the stamp impression are traced.

The identification of individual stamps is much easier on tiles with more elaborate designs, since the chances of two stamps producing a more or less identically spaced pattern are remote. Several different and widely spaced points of the stamp need to be identical before it can be said that the tiles were decorated using the same stamp. Simple patterns and small stamps (see page 29 below) are more difficult because of the ease with which a very close copy of the design could have been made.

The need for accuracy and caution in declaring tiles to have been made from the same stamps must be emphasised. This is because statements about stamps are extremely important in the interpretation of the industry, and because so many mistakes have been made in the past. To reiterate: the paramount need in discussion of tiles is to be clear as to whether it is the stamps or merely the designs which are said to be the same. *It is not possible to identify stamps from reduced (ie, published) drawings of designs.*

Allocating design numbers
It has been noted that occasionally more than one stamp might bear the same design. How similar do the stamps have to be allocated to the same design number? When a drawing of a tile design is published it will be reduced to 1:3. As a rule of thumb, if the differences between two stamps are more than just spacing, and can be illustrated in a published drawing, then they should be treated as two different designs. If the differences between the stamps cannot be shown in a reduced drawing, they should be treated as two stamps of the same design.

The characteristics of stamps are not the only problem in deciding when to assign a new design number. Badly worn, or fragmentary tiles cause further difficulties. The same rules apply here as when deciding between two stamps: that is, are the differences on the tiles under consideration demonstrable in a published drawing? If they are, separate design numbers should be allocated. If not, it is possible that the differences are only a result of poor quality manufacture (smearing of part of the design, perhaps), and further examples are needed before another design number is allocated.

Identifying designs on fragments
Where it is difficult to identify the design on a fragment, it can be helpful to make a quick tracing and to compare this with 1:1 drawings, or complete tiles. Where fragments are very small, or extremely worn, and the visible remains of the design are of a very common type, record the design as **Don't Know**. Scored and split tiles are treated like fragments, and given the same design number as whole tiles of their design.

3.3 Recording decorated floor tiles

Notes on using the recording form for decorated tiles (Fig 10):
1. *Tile no*: Give each tile or fragment a unique number. Where two fragments fit together and so definitely came from the same tile, give them the same number and record them as one tile. Record: **Tile 1, T2, T3**, *etc*.
2. *Design No*: Give each design a number. See notes above about allocating design numbers. Where the design in question is part of an interlocking pattern that uses several tiles together, give the whole arrangement the same design number, but use suffixes (for example '24a', '24b', '24c') to distinguish between individual tile designs. Record: **Design 1, D2, D3a, D3b**, *etc*.
3. *Group No*: The production group number. See notes on pages 2–3 on assigning tiles to production groups. Leave blank if a group number has not yet been allocated. Record: **Production Group 1, PG2, PG3**, *etc*.
4. *Site*: The site where the tiles were found.
5. *Provenance now*: Where the tiles are now stored. Give full details of where they are stored. If they are *in situ*, say whereabouts they are in the building: *eg*, **S**outh **T**ransept. Keep a record of any abbreviations used.
6. *Context/Phasing*: Put any contextual information here. If the tile is *in situ* record as **IS**.

Shape and size (See general points on pages 6–8).
7. *Shape*: What shape was/is the complete tile?
   If there is not enough of the tile present to be certain of the shape — for example that it is definitely a square and not a rectangle — put **D**on't **K**now. Record: **SQ**uare, **TRI**angle, **REC**tangle, **D**on't **K**now.
8. *Depth*: Give the depth of the tile in mm. Depth can be recorded for all except spalled fragments. Where the depth of the tile is uneven, choose an average point.
9. *Fragment code*: Tiles with depth as their only complete measurement are given a fragment code. This is an 'not more than' measure of the surface area of the fragment. Codes for different sized fragments are shown in Figure 3. Where the fragment is irregularly shaped, estimate the relevant code. Record: **A, B, C**, *etc*.
10. *Upper Surface Long*: Give the longer complete upper surface measurement, if there is one, in mm.
11. *Upper Surface Short*: Give the shorter complete upper surface measurement, if there is one, in mm.
12. *Upper Surface One*: Where there is only one complete measurement, put it here.

Upper Surface
13. *Scored*: Has the upper surface of the tile been cut part way through the depth of the tile? See Plate 1. Record: **Y**es, **N**o, **D**on't **K**now.

1. TILE NO _____ 2. DESIGN NO _____ 3. GROUP NO _____
4. SITE _____ 5. PROVENANCE NOW _____
6. CONTEXT/PHASING _____

Shape and Size

7. SHAPE _____ 8. DEPTH _____ 9. FRAG _____
10. USLONG _____ 11. USSHORT _____ 12. USONE _____

Upper Surface

13. SCORED _____ 14. SPLIT _____
15. NAIL HOLES _____ 16. DISTANCE _____
17. DECORATIVE TECHNIQUE _____
18. GLAZE ON BODY FABRIC _____ & ON WHITE CLAY _____
19. DAMAGE _____ 20. GRADE WEAR _____
21. STAMP NO _____ 22. STAMP _____

Sides and Core

23. ANGLE OF BEVEL _____ 24. FABRIC CODE _____
25. FIRING _____

Lower Surface

26. SANDY _____ 27. KEYS _____

Comments: _____

Fig 10 Decorated floor tile recording form (see also template in back pocket)

14 *Split*: Have one or more sides of the tile been broken to make a triangle or small square or small rectangle? See Plate 2. Record: **Yes, No, Don't Know**.
15 *Nail holes*: Are there any nail holes in the corners or centre of the tile?
    See general points on pages 8–10 and Plate 3 for information on how to recognise nail holes. Record the number of holes, whether they are in adjacent or diagonal corners, and/or the centre of the tile. For example: **1COR**ner, **2ADJ**acent, **2DIA**gonal, **3ADJ**acent+**1CEN**tre, **No**, **Do**n't **Know**.

    Only record the number of nail holes you can actually see on each tile or fragment. Put **Don't Know** if it is not clear. Nail holes are uncommon in decorated tiles, but do occur.
16 *Distance*: Where there are nail holes in the corner(s) of the tile, give the range of the distance from the corners to the nail holes in mm. See the points on page 10 on how to record this.
    Recording examples:
        5 *ie*, the hole/s is/are up to 5mm from the corner
        5–10 *ie*, the holes are between 5 and 10mm from the corner
        10–25 *ie*, the holes are between 10 and 25mm from the corner
17 *Decorative technique*: The technique used to decorate the tile. See notes at the beginning of the section on recording decorated tiles and all the Plates. Also bear in mind the general notes on recording descriptive variables and unusual characteristics on pages 5–6. Use an oblique sign where you are unsure which of two techniques have been used. Use a plus sign where more than one technique has been used. Record:
        Stamped & Slipped + depth of slip in mm
        Inlaid + depth of inlay in mm
        2 PLANE Relief
        MODELled Relief
        2 PLANE Counter Relief
        MODELled Counter Relief
        Line IMPressed + depth of impression in mm.
    For the more unusual techniques, record:
        S OVER S + depth of slip in mm
        REVERSE S & S + depth of slip in mm
        REVERSE Inlay + depth in mm
        Slip Painted
        Hand INCised
    Where it is not clear which technique was used, record:
        S & S/I + depth of white clay in mm
        Slip Decorated + depth of slip in mm
        L IMP/CR
        R/CR
18 *Glaze on the body fabric*: Give the colour any remains of glaze has fired to over the body fabric of the tile. Record: **BL**ack, **BR**own, **C**ream, **G**reen **D**ark, **G**reen **L**ight, **OL**ive, **OR**ange, **P**urple brown, **Y**ellow, **D**on't **K**now.
    These abbreviations follow Eames' catalogue of tiles in the British

Museum (1980, I, 286). Be wary of using **Cream**; check that the slip doesn't just look cream because the glaze has worn off. Put **Don't Know** if the tile is too worn to tell the colour of the glaze. If the tile is streaked or spotted so that more than one colour is present, put both: *eg* **Y + BR** or **Y + GL**, *etc.*

Glaze on the white clay: Give the colour any remains of glaze has fired to over white clay on the upper surface of the tile. Record (after Eames 1980, I, 286): **BR**own Light, **Cream, G**reen **L**ight, **OL**ive, **OR**ange, **Y**ellow, **D**on't **K**now, **NONE**.

Put **Don't Know** if the tile is too worn to tell the colour of the glaze. Put **NONE** if the whole upper surface of the tile is glazed without any white clay. If more than one colour is present, put both.

19 *Damage*: Was the tile faulted in any particular way during its production?

When filling in this category bear the general points on recording descriptive variables in mind (see pages 5 – 6 and Pl 11). Consistency is important here. The following are some possible categories of damage and recording abbreviations:

SLIP/INLAY — the slip or inlay has cracked and/or shrunk away from the body fabric and/or flaked off or fallen out
SLip **UNEVEN** — the slip has a bumpy surface
SMEARed — the slip either does not cover, or is not confined to the impressed parts of the tile
BLOTchy — the glaze has left black spots on the upper surface
SANDy — sand on the upper surface before firing
PACKing lines — cracks in the fabric which show right through to the lower surface, suggesting that several lumps of clay have been pressed together
WARPed — the tile is warped
WASTER — the tile is so badly damaged it could not have been used in a floor. Be careful about using this — very poor tiles are known to have been used. The presence of any mortar or wear marks should be looked for
None
Don't Know

20 *Wear*: Grade the degree of wear on the tile. Use the following as approximate guidelines, and see the Plates as examples:
    1 All the slip and more than 75% of the glaze is present on the tile or fragment
    2 More than 50% of the glaze and 75% of the slip is present
    3 Less than 25% of the glaze, but more than 50% of the slip is present
    4 Less than 25% of the slip and no glaze is present.

21 *Stamp No*: Where a particular stamp can be recognised, give it a number with the prefix **SN**, so that there is no confusion with other number series such as mosaic shapes. See notes about stamps on pages 21 – 22.

22 *Stamp*: Give details of any particular features of the stamp here. See notes about stamps on pages 21–22, and on small stamps on page 29, and see Plate 9 for an example of a cracked stamp. For example, record:
    CRACKed
    SMALL stamp x number of times used on the tile.

Sides and core

23 *Angle of bevel*: Are the sides of the tile vertical, sloped at less than 7°, or more than 7°? See page 8 for general points. Use Figure 4 (back pocket) as a template to check if the angle is more or less than 7°. Record: **VE**rtical, **SL**ightly bevelled — *ie* less than 7°, **ST**eeply bevelled — *ie* more than 7°.

24 *Fabric code*: Fabric can only be recorded from tile fragments with a clean, broken edge. See notes on page 5. Each fabric type should be described as set out below. The allotted fabric code is then used in the recording form. Delete or fill in as applicable:

Fabric Code _____
Texture: LAMINATED/WELL MIXED   Fracture: SMOOTH/JAGGED
Hardness: HARD/AVERAGE/SOFT
Inclusions: **QUARTZ**   SIZE: _____   FREQ: _____
Other: _____ SIZE: _____   FREQ: _____
Other: _____ SIZE: _____   FREQ: _____
Comment: _____

    Fabric is *soft* if it can be scratched with a fingernail, *average* if it can be scratched by metal, or *hard* if it cannot be scratched by metal. Use the abbreviation **LT** for less than, and **MT** for more than; the symbols < and > are too often confused. Use Figure 6 to estimate frequency and record the relevant percentages. Record inclusion size as a range: for example 1–2mm, 1–10mm, Less Than 1mm, *etc*.

25 *Firing*: Tiles fired in the presence of oxygen are said to be 'oxidised', and their fabric is pink or red. Tiles fired in an atmosphere where oxygen is excluded are said to be 'reduced', and their fabric is grey or black. Many tiles are partly oxidised and partly reduced. The degree of oxidisation is a good group indicator. Be careful about only recording what you actually know about each tile or fragment. Record:
        OXidised — fabric is red or pink at surfaces and core
        REDuced — fabric is grey or black at surfaces and core
        CORE REDuced — surfaces are oxidised but the core is reduced
        OXidised **SURF**ace**S** — all surfaces oxidised, core unknown
        Upper Surface **PATCHY** — the upper surface is partly reduced, the rest of the tile sides are oxidised
        Upper Surface **RED**uced — lower surface and sides oxidised, but

upper surface reduced
Don't Know

Lower Surface
26 *Sand*: Has the tile got sand on its base? Record: **Yes**, **No**, **Don't Know**.
27 *Keys*: Have any keys been cut into the lower surface of the tile?
Any part of the lower surface that has been cut away is recorded here. A variety of keys are illustrated by Ponsonby and Ponsonby (1934, 33). For recording purposes the abbreviations used by Eames (1980, I, 286) in the catalogue of tiles in the British Museum are followed here, with one alteration: 'Bevel' is replaced by 'pared' in order to avoid confusion with the bevelled sides in category 23. **Pared** means that the edges of the base of the tile have been cut away as shown in Figure 7; the number present means the number of edges which are pared in this way. **Rebate** is a piece of clay cut out along one of the base edges (see Fig 8). Rebates are usually restricted to rectangular tiles thought to be made for use as step risers.

Record as follows and draw a rough sketch of one of the keys in plan and section as, for example, shown in Figure 9:
> **SC**ooped + number present
> **ST**abbed **R**ound + number present
> **ST**abbed **S**quare + number present
> **PARED** + number present
> **X** — a cross is cut in the base of the tile
> **REBATE**
> None
> Don't Know

3.4 Mosaic Floor Tiles

From the point of view of recording, mosaic tiles combine features of both plain and decorated tiles. Some mosaic tiles have no design on their upper surface; rather they rely on the interlocking of the mosaic shapes, and the alternation of light and dark colours to achieve their decorative effect. However, other mosaic tiles are decorated. Consequently there are two sections of the recording form for the upper surface: one of these refers only to decorated mosaic tiles, and can be ignored for the rest. For the terminology and methods of recording decoration see pages 18–21 above. Use the same tile and design number series for decorated mosaic tiles as used for other decorated tiles. Additional points, particularly relevant to mosaic tiles, are discussed below.

Small stamps
Most stamps are more or less the same size as the quarry upon which they are used. Small stamps are considerably smaller than their quarries, and are often of a single, simple motif, such as a rosette. They are most frequently used to decorate mosaic tiles, and the designs are usually line impressed. There is some

argument that small stamps with line impression designs may have been made of metal rather than wood, but this remains uncertain. Slip decorated and inlaid designs are also known to have been made using small stamps.

Identifying and recording small stamps

The same small stamp may be used several times on the same tile, or in combination with other small stamps. Eames discusses a line impressed example on a square tile from Pipewell Abbey (Eames 1980, I, 40–3, pl viiia). This tile was stamped with four outlines of a hound. Tracings showed that although the hound outline was identical throughout, the distance between the four hounds varied on different tiles, demonstrating that a small stamp had been used.

If you are sure that a small stamp has been used, record category 13 as: **SMALL** stamp x number of times used on the tile. If more than one small stamp has been used, put both stamp numbers in category 12. Give a design number to the total pattern on the upper surface — *ie*, to the use of the two stamps together. If they are used in different combinations on other tiles, give each of these combinations a separate design number.

Recording unusual types of mosaic tile

Bear in mind the notes on recording unusual techniques on page 5.

Most mosaic pieces are manufactured in the shape they are intended for use. Rarely, mosaic panels have been made from scoring and splitting square tiles into simple mosaic shapes. This is not recorded as a separate decorative technique here; the number of scored and split sides on each tile is noted in category 24.

The term *pseudo-mosaic* usually refers to tiles which have been scored with a shallow line, not intended for splitting, but to give the effect of a mosaic pavement. For this reason the depth of scoring on mosaic tiles which have and have not been split is recorded to enable comparisons to be made.

Size and shape

The size and shape of mosaic tiles are recorded differently from other types of tiles. This is because, depth apart, mosaic tiles do not have easily definable points between which measurements can be taken. However, numbered drawings of a good range of mosaic outlines have been published at 1:2 in the British Museum's catalogue of medieval tiles (Eames 1980, II, S1-S328). Full size replicas of these can be used as templates, and the numbers allocated by Eames and prefixed 'S', can be used for recording purposes. Each of these templates must be seen as the average of a range. Any tiles which fall more than 5mm outside this average should be recorded and published separately as a new shape, with a new shape number. Pay particular attention to broken edges and scored and split sides when dealing with mosaic tile. They are easily missed. Broken edges can be misleading when recording shape, and scored and split sides can suggest links between two or more shapes.

Mosaic number

The recording of mosaics requires two numbered series more than those used for recording other types of tile. Both of these follow series provided by Eames' catalogue (1980, II). The shape series has already been discussed. The mosaic arrangement series uses Roman numerals (Eames 1980, II, i-lxxix). It refers to the overall arrangement of tile shapes used together in a pavement. Mosaic numbers should only be assigned where it is certain that the tiles being recorded were used together in that way.

The mosaic number series should not be confused with the production group number. Several mosaic arrangements might be part of the same production group, or alternatively a mosaic arrangement might form part of a production group with other types of tiles.

3.5 Recording Mosaic Tiles

Notes on using the recording form for mosaic tiles (Fig 11):
1. *Site*: The site where the tiles were found.
2. *Provenance now*: Where the tiles are now stored. If they are *in situ*, put whereabouts in the building they are: *eg*, **South Transept**, *etc*. Keep a record of any abbreviations used.
3. *Number of tiles* described by this record. See notes on page 3 on recording tiles individually or not. Where the record is of an individual tile, put **1**. Where the record is for a group of tiles put the number of whole tiles and the number of fragments.
4. *Group Number*: The production group number. See notes on pages 2–3 on assigning tiles to production groups. Leave blank if a group number has not yet been allocated. Record: **Production Group 1**, **PG2**, **PG3**, *etc*.
5. *Mosaic Number*: Give the mosaic arrangement number for this tile/tiles if known. See notes above. Use and add to Eames' series of mosaic arrangement numbers as published in the British Museum catalogue (1980, II). Record: Mosaic **I**, **XL**, **LXIX**, *etc*. Do not use a prefix ('M') in this case as it may become confused as part of the Roman numeral.
6. *Context/Phasing*: Record any contextual information here. If the tile was found *in situ* record as **IS**.

Shape and Size (see general points on pages 6–7).
7. *Shape*: What shape was/is the complete tile? Be sure that there is enough of the tile present to be certain of the shape. If you don't know, put **Don't Know**. Record: **Shape 1**, **S2**, **S328**, **Don't Know**.
8. *From*: If the tile has been scored and split from a larger tile, give the shape of the parent tile. Record: **S32**, **S279**.
9. *Depth*: Record the depth of the tile in mm. Depth can be recorded for all except spalled tiles. Where the depth of the tile is uneven, choose an average point.

1. SITE _____   2. PROVENANCE NOW _____
3. NO OF TILES _____ 4. GROUP NO _____ 5. MOSAIC NO _____
6. CONTEXT/PHASING _____

Shape and Size
7. SHAPE _____ 8. FROM _____ 9. DEPTH _____

Upper Surface (if decorated)
10. TILE _____ 11. DESIGN _____ 12. STAMP NO _____
13. STAMP _____ 14. TECHNIQUE _____

Upper Surface (all tiles)
15. SLIP _____ 16. GLAZE _____
17. NAIL HOLES _____ 18. DISTANCE _____
19. DAMAGE _____ 20. WEAR _____

Sides and Core
21. SIDES _____ 22. ANGLE OF BEVEL _____
23. SCORED _____ 24. SPLIT _____
25. ASSEMBLY MARKS _____
26. FIRING _____ 27. FABRIC CODE _____

Lower Surface
28. SANDY _____ 29. KEYS _____

Comments: _____

Fig 11 Mosaic floor tile recording form (see also template in back pocket)

Upper Surface (if decorated)
This section only applies to decorated mosaic tiles.
10 *Tile No*: Give each tile or fragment a unique number. Where two fragments fit together and so definitely came from the same tile, give them the same number and record them as one tile. Where mosaic tiles are being recorded alongside decorated tiles, use the same tile number series for the two types of tiles. Record: **Tile 1, T2, T3,** *etc.*
11 *Design No*: Give each design a number. See notes above on pages 22 – 3 about allocating design numbers. Where mosaic tiles are being recorded alongside decorated tiles, use the same design number series for the two types of tiles. Record: **Design 1, D2, D3,** *etc.*
12 *Stamp No*: Where a particular stamp can be recognised, give it a number with the prefix **SN**, so that there is no confusion with other number series such as mosaic shapes. See notes about stamps on pages 21 – 2. Where mosaic tiles are being recorded alongside decorated tiles, use the same stamp number series throughout. Record: **SN1, SN2,** *etc.*
13 *Stamp*: Give details of any particular features of the stamp here. See notes about stamps on pages 21 – 2, and on small stamps on page 29, and see Plate 9 for an example of a cracked stamp. For example, record:
    CRACKed
    SMALL stamp x number of times used on the tile.
14 *Decorative technique*: The technique used to decorate the tile. See notes at the beginning of the previous section on recording decorated tiles (pages 19 – 21) and bear in mind the general notes on recording descriptive variables and unusual characteristics on pages 5 – 6. Only the abbreviations for decorative techniques already known on mosaic tiles have been repeated here. Use an oblique sign where it is uncertain which of two techniques have been used. Use a plus sign where more than one technique has been used. Record:
    Stamped & Slipped + depth of slip in mm
    Inlaid + depth of inlay in mm
    Line IMPressed + depth of impression
    Counter Relief
For the more unusual techniques, record:
    REVERSE S & S + depth of slip in mm
    REVERSE Inlay + depth in mm
    Hand INCised

Upper Surface (all tiles)
15 *Slip*: Is there any white clay on the upper surface of the tile? If the tile is too worn to tell put **Don't Know**. Record: **Yes, No, Don't Know.**
16 *Glaze*: What colour has the glaze on the upper surface of the tile fired to? Record: **BL**ack, **BR**own, **C**ream, **G**reen **D**ark, **G**reen **L**ight, **OL**ive, **OR**ange, **P**urple brown, **Y**ellow, **D**on't **K**now.

These abbreviations follow Eames' catalogue of tiles in the British Museum (1980, I, 286). If the tile is too worn to tell the colour of the glaze put **Don't Know**. If the tile has fired to one colour over areas of white clay, and another colour over the body fabric, put both with a plus sign between: *eg*, **Y+BR** or **Y+GD**, *etc*.

17 *Nail holes*: Are there any nail holes in the corners or centre of the tile?

See the general points on pages 8–10 and Plate 3 for information on recording and recognising nail holes. Record the number of holes, whether they are in adjacent or diagonal corners, and/or the centre of the tile. For example: 1**COR**ner, 2**ADJ**acent, 2**DIA**gonal, 3**ADJ**acent+1**CEN**tre, No, **Don't Know**.

Only record the number of nail holes you can actually see on each tile or fragment. Put **Don't Know** if it is not clear.

18 *Distance*: Where there are nail holes in the corner(s) of the tile, give the range of the distance from the corners to the nail holes. See the general points on page 10 for how to record this. Recording examples:

    5 *ie*, the hole/s is/are up to 5mm from the corner
    5–10 *ie*, the holes are between 5 and 10mm from the corner
    10–25 *ie*, the holes are between 10 and 25mm from the corner

19 *Damage*: Was the tile faulted in any particular way during its production?

When filling in this category bear the general points on recording descriptive variables in mind (see pages 5–6 and Pl 11). Consistency is important here. The following are some possible categories of damage and recording abbreviations:

    SLip **UNEVEN** — the slip has a bumpy surface
    SMEARed — the slip either does not cover, or is not confined to the impressed parts of the tile
    BLOTchy — the glaze has left black spots on the upper surface
    SANDy — sand on the upper surface before firing
    PACKing lines — cracks in the fabric which show right through to the lower surface, suggesting that several lumps of clay have been pressed together
    WARPed — the tile is warped
    WASTER — the tile is so badly damaged it could not have been used in a floor. Be careful about using this — very poor tiles are known to have been used. The presence of any mortar or wear marks should be looked for.
    None
    Don't Know

20 *Wear*: Grade the degree of wear on the tile. Use the following as approximate guidelines, and the Plates as examples:

    1 All the slip and more than 75% of the glaze is present on the tile or fragment
    2 More than 50% of the glaze and 75% of the slip is present

    3 Less than 25% of the glaze, but more than 50% of the slip is present
    4 Less than 25% of the slip and no glaze is present

Sides and Core

21 *Sides*: How have the sides of the tiles been treated? The curved sides of mosaic tiles can sometimes be seen to form several planes, where they have been cut out or **TRIM**med with a knife. This has been illustrated by Beaulah (1929, 119, fig 12). Record: **TRIM**med, **N**one, **D**on't **K**now.

22 *Angle of Bevel*: Are the sides of the tile vertical, sloped at less than 7°, or more than 7°? See page 8 for general points. Use Figure 4 (back pocket) as a template to check if the angle is more or less than 7°. Record:
        VErtical
        SLightly bevelled — *ie*, less than 7°
        STeeply bevelled — *ie*, more than 7°.

23 *Scored*: Has the upper surface of the tile been cut part way through the depth of the tile? See notes on page 29, and Plate 1. Record: **Y**es + the depth of the scoring, **N**o, **D**on't **K**now.

24 *Split*: Have one or more sides of the tile been scored and then broken to make smaller tiles? See notes on pages 29–30 and Plate 2. Record the number of sides that are scored and split, and the average depth of the scoring in mm. For example: **2 + 5mm**, **N**o, **D**on't **K**now.

25 *Assembly Marks*: Are there any assembly marks on the sides of the tile? Mosaic tiles were sometimes marked with Roman numerals or other 'assembly marks' to help those laying the tiles put them in the right order. Record: **Y**es and give a sketch of the marks, **N**o, **D**on't **K**now.

26 *Firing*: Tiles fired in the presence of oxygen are said to be 'oxidised', and their fabric is pink or red. Tiles fired in an atmosphere where oxygen is excluded are said to be 'reduced', and their fabric is grey or black. Many tiles are partly oxidised and partly reduced. Record:
        OXidised — fabric is red or pink at surfaces and core
        REDuced — fabric is grey or black at surfaces and core
        CORE REDuced — surfaces are oxidised but the core is reduced
        OXidised **SURF**ace**S** — all surfaces oxidised, core unknown
        Upper Surface **PATCHY** — the upper surface is partly reduced, the rest of the tile sides are oxidised
        Upper Surface **RED**uced — lower surface and sides oxidised, but upper surface reduced
        Don't **K**now

27 *Fabric code*: Fabric can only be recorded from tile fragments with a clean, broken edge. See notes on page 5. Each fabric type should be described as set out below. The allotted fabric code is then used in the recording form. Delete or fill in as applicable:

Fabric Code _____ Texture:
LAMINATED/WELL MIXED   Fracture: SMOOTH/JAGGED
Hardness: HARD/AVERAGE/SOFT
Inclusions: **QUARTZ**   SIZE: _____   FREQ: _____
Other: _____   SIZE: _____   FREQ: _____
Other: _____   SIZE: _____   FREQ: _____
Comment: _____

Fabric is *soft* if it can be scratched with a fingernail, *average* if it can be scratched by metal, or *hard* if it cannot be scratched by metal. Use the abbreviation **LT** for less than, and **MT** for more than; the symbols < and > are too often confused. Use Figure 6 to estimate frequency and record the relevant percentages. Record inclusion size as a range: for example 1–2mm, 1–10mm, Less Than 1mm, *etc.*

Lower Surface
28 *Sandy*: Has the tile got sand on its base? Record: **Y**es, **N**o, **D**on't **K**now.
29 *Keys*: Have any keys been cut into the lower surface of the tile?
Any part of the lower surface that has been cut away is recorded here. A variety of keys are illustrated by Ponsonby and Ponsonby (1934, 33). For recording purposes the abbreviations used by Eames (1980, I, 286) in the catalogue of tiles in the British Museum are followed here with one alteration. 'Bevel' is replaced by 'pared' in order to avoid confusion with the bevelled sides in category 23. **Pared** means that the edges of the base of the tile have been cut away as shown in Figure 7; the number present means the number of edges which are pared in this way. **Rebate** is a piece of clay cut out along one of the base edges (see Fig 8). Rebates are usually restricted to rectangular tiles thought to be made for use as step risers. Record as follows and draw a rough sketch of one of the keys in plan and section as, for example, shown in Figure 9:
  SCooped + number present
  STabbed **R**ound + number present
  STabbed **S**quare + number present
  PARED + number present
  X — a cross is cut in the base of the tile
  REBATE
  None
  Don't **K**now

4 Publishing

4.1 Introduction

This section is intended to identify matters concerning publication which arise from the use of this recording system, or which cause particular problems when trying to use reports.

Once the tiles have been allocated to production groups (as discussed on pages 2–3) draw up a summary of the characteristics which identify each group. Publish the tiles and the design drawings in these groups as follows:

1. Give the number of tiles and the number of fragments for each group, and a statement of the recording methodology followed.
2. Set out the characteristics for each group of tiles in a standardised way. Include all the recorded variables. Give both the mean and range of dimensions. Where a characteristic varies within a group, give full details, unless the variation is just a single odd tile. Use percentages or numbers of tiles to show the proportion of tiles involved for each variation.
3. Explain what makes each group a production group; that is, specify the reasons why a group of tiles belong together and what makes it different from others.
4. Where comparisons are made between decorated tiles of similar or the same design, be clear about whether it is the designs or the stamps which are being compared.

4.2 Drawing designs

All design drawings are idealised to some extent. The same designs were generally used on large numbers of tiles. Through differences in manufacture and wear these tiles will differ from one another. Each design drawing has to represent the design from all those tiles. Consequently, variations caused by damage in manufacture or later, or by wear, have to be recognised and ignored. At the same time, however, it is the aim of design drawings to represent the design as accurately as possible.

To achieve this apparently contradictory aim it is important to use as many tiles or fragments as possible to work out the design, while at the same time being careful not to 'invent' any of it. Where there are no complete examples of a design, draw only what can be seen on the extant fragments, even if you are 'sure' that the design was symmetrical. Drawing the designs of stamped and slipped tiles can be particularly difficult. The spread of slip can vary considerably on different tiles of the same design. 'Accidental' variations can more easily be recognised and ignored if several examples are used.

Some conventions have been established to illustrate the different techniques used in tile decoration. The major problem with these is that there is no established method for showing areas in which the design cannot be ascertained. The drawing of a stamped and slipped tile, for example, will show the slipped part of the tile as perfectly white and the body fabric as black. Where part of the tile is too worn or damaged to tell whether it was slipped or not this area has usually been illustrated as black (Fig 12 a, b). This is very misleading. It is important for the recorder to show on the drawing the areas of design which both are, and are not, known. On a slip decorated tile this means the drawing has to make clear the parts of the tile where the tile was glazed dark over the body fabric, the parts where the tile was glazed light over the slip, and the parts where the distinction between light and dark cannot be recognised. Figure 12, c and d shows designs stippled over the areas which are not known. Drawings done in this way may not superficially look as good as those of the traditional kind, but they provide a much better record of the medieval material.

It is clear, then, that design drawings are not drawings of a particular tile. In some cases, where the differences between two stamps cannot be illustrated on a reduced drawing, they may be made up from tiles with designs produced by different stamps. For this reason, and because a reduced drawing does not give the kind of detail necessary to recognise individual stamps, design drawings cannot be used to identify tiles made with the same stamps.

Recommended conventions

a Designs should be drawn at 1:1 and reduced to 1:3 for publication. This is a considerable reduction. The best results are obtained by using pens of not less than 0.5mm. Stipple needs to be very sparse on the original.

b Publish mosaic shapes at 1:1 if possible so that they can be used as templates in comparative studies. Indicate whether the outline is of the upper or lower surface of the tile and which, if any, sides are scored and split.

c Use a thick line for a complete tile edge, and a thinner line for broken ones.

d Draw designs which are known from antiquarian drawings, but for which there are no extant examples, in outline only using a broken line.

There is no need to publish sections, since depth, keys, angle of bevel, *etc*, are included in the recording system.

The following are suggestions for drawing different decorative techniques. As areas of black, white and stipple mean different things for different techniques, it is important to say what technique is being illustrated.

Slip decorated or inlaid
Ink areas of glaze on the body fabric in black. Leave areas of glaze over slip or inlay white. Stipple areas where the design cannot be discerned.

Relief and counter relief
Graded stipple has conventionally been used to show relief tiles but is only really successful with designs in high, modelled relief. Lower and two-plane relief tiles are better illustrated by outlining the design in a solid black line and using a sparse, even stipple over all the *depressed* areas (see Fig 12e).

Fig 12 Comparison of drawing techniques. a) and b): *the same design; in* a) *the design could not be clearly seen;* c) and d) *are examples of design drawings in which stipple has been used to indicate areas where the design is not clear;* e) *stipple used to show the depressed area of a counter relief design*

Line impressed
Use thick solid black lines to show the impression, and leave the background white regardless of the colour of the glaze.

4.3 Recording whole pavements and tiles *in situ*

Photographs

Small areas of tile can easily be planned by hand. However, where large areas are involved, scaled or rectified photographs are an extremely useful way of recording *in situ* tiles. All such photographic work should be done in colour: black and white film is insufficiently responsive to the difference between worn tiles and some of those that are slipped and glazed.

Plans

Where tiles are in good condition, and all the required information is clearly shown on the photographs, drawings of the layout of a pavement may not be necessary. The prints can be cut out and assembled to form a montage. This is particularly effective when dealing with large areas of mosaic tile. A location plan will also be required.

Drawings are necessary where the condition of the tiles is such that designs or differences in glaze are not clearly shown in the photographs. Tile outlines can be traced off the scaled photographs and the resulting plans used for recording further information. This information should include the shape of the tiles, the colour of the glaze if they are plain, the design and its orientation if they are decorated, and whether tiles have been scored across the upper surface. It is not necessary to show the condition of tiles in these drawings; this will be clear from the photographs. However, where drawings are published without accompanying photographs it is important to show where tiles are too worn to know whether they were originally decorated or plain.

In some instances an extra drawing may be desirable giving an interpretation of the original condition or layout of a pavement. This is frequently the case when dealing with mosaic because the regularity of these pavements can be reconstructed from a few tiles. For example, where part of a roundel has been found, the design of the rest of the roundel can be suggested with reasonable confidence, and the overall size estimated. In these circumstances an extra drawing is also desirable because mosaic depends for its effect on showing large numbers of tiles together.

5 References

The main reference work for all aspects of medieval floor tiles is Elizabeth Eames' *Catalogue of medieval lead-glazed earthenware tiles in the Department of Medieval and Later Antiquities, British Museum* (1980, vols I & II). The British Museum has also published a paperback on *English Medieval Tiles* by Elizabeth Eames (1985). This small and inexpensive volume contains a great deal of information and excellent illustrations, plus a useful reference section including a list of sites and museums with medieval tiles on display. Information and bulletins concerning the *Census of Medieval Tiles* can be obtained from Dr E C Norton at the Centre for Medieval Studies, University of York, King's Manor, York YO1 2EP. Other publications which have been mentioned, or which discuss unusual aspects of manufacture or decoration are:

Beaulah, G K, 1929   Paving tiles from Meaux Abbey, Appendix to T Sheppard, Meaux Abbey, *Trans East Riding Antiq Soc* **26**, 116-36

Drury, P J, 1979   Techniques of decoration and their distribution, in synopsis of the *Cambridge seminar on medieval floor tiles*, held 24-6 November 1978, 9-11

Hirst, S M, Walsh, D, & Wright, S M, 1983   *Bordesley Abbey II: second report on excavations at Bordesley Abbey, Redditch, Hereford-Worcestershire*, Oxford, Brit Archaeol Rep **111**

Knight, S, & Keen, L, 1977   Medieval floor tiles from Guisborough Priory, Yorkshire, *Yorkshire Archaeol J* **49**, 65-75

Norton, E C, 1984   Guidelines for the recording and publication of medieval tiles, in synopsis of the *London seminar for the Census of Medieval Tiles*, held 30th November 1984

Peacock, D P S, 1977   Ceramics in Roman and medieval archaeology, in D P S Peacock, (ed), *Pottery and early commerce*, London, 21-33

Ponsonby Lord, & Ponsonby, M, 1934   Monastic paving tiles, *Sussex Archaeol Collect* **75**, 19-64

Stopford, J, 1990   *The changing structure of a small medieval industry: an approach to the study of floor tiles*, unpubl PhD thesis, University of Reading

Plate 1 A stamped and slipped tile which was scored diagonally before firing to make two triangles, but which was not subsequently broken. Note that in the DAMAGE category, this tile would be recorded as BLOTCHY. WEAR = 1

Plate 2 A stamped and slipped tile which has been split from a scored square. Note the smoothness of the cut surface and the roughness of the broken one. WEAR = 1

Plate 3 A hand incised tile. The slip has been scraped away so that the glaze on the tile body fabric makes the dark lettering, against a light, slipped background. Note the guidelines incised through the slip to keep the lettering even. These emphasise the laborious nature of this type of decoration and should be included in a design drawing. Also note the nail holes in the three corners of the tile. WEAR = 3

Plate 4 Hand incised tiles. WEAR = 2

Plate 5 A hexagonal tile inlaid with about 2mm of white clay. WEAR = 1

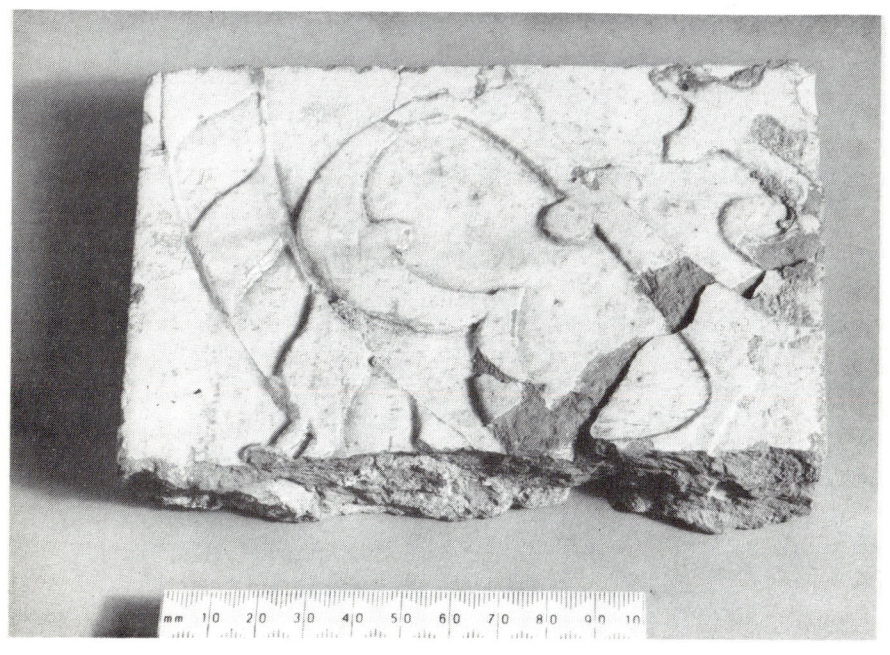

Plate 6 A two-plane relief decorated tile. WEAR = 1. There is a published photograph of a modelled relief tile in Eames (1980, I, pl viiib)

Plate 7 A two-plane counter relief tile. WEAR = 1

Plate 8 A line impressed fragment. WEAR = 2 or 3

Plate 9 A stamped and slipped tile made with a cracked stamp. Note the effect this has: the body fabric is flush where there is no slip, but the crack in the raised parts of the stamp leaves a ridge across the parts of the tile that are meant to be impressed and slip decorated. WEAR = 2 or 3

Plate 11 The smeared design of this stamped and slipped tile would make a stamp tracing impossible and a design drawing difficult. Note also the sand on the upper surface before firing. Smear and sand would both be recorded in the DAMAGE section. WEAR, however, = 1

Plate 10 Overleaf. These two tiles are decorated with the same design, probably *made with the same stamp.* However, they belong to different (albeit linked) production groups because the quarries are different sizes (b is larger) and different decorative techniques were used. b is stamped and slipped to a depth of less than 0.5mm, a is inlaid to more than 1mm

NOTES